WEEKLY  READER®
EARLY LEARNING LIBRARY

My Day at School

In the Classroom

by Joanne Mattern

Reading consultant: Susan Nations, M.Ed.,
author/literacy coach/
consultant in literacy development

Please visit our web site at: www.garethstevens.com
For a free color catalog describing Weekly Reader® Early Learning Library's list
of high-quality books, call 1-877-445-5824 (USA) or 1-800-387-3178 (Canada).
Weekly Reader® Early Learning Library's fax: (414) 336-0164.

Library of Congress Cataloging-in-Publication Data

Mattern, Joanne, 1963-
   In the classroom / by Joanne Mattern.
     p. cm. — (My day at school)
   Includes bibliographical references and index.
   ISBN-10: 0-8368-6787-4 — ISBN-13: 978-0-8368-6787-9 (lib. bdg.)
   ISBN-10: 0-8368-6794-7 — ISBN-13: 978-0-8368-6794-7 (softcover)
   1. Classroom environment—Juvenile literature.   2. School children—Juvenile literature.
 I. Title.
 LC210.M38   2006
 372.18—dc22   2006005138

This edition first published in 2007 by
Weekly Reader® Early Learning Library
A Member of the WRC Media Family of Companies
330 West Olive Street, Suite 100
Milwaukee, WI 53212 USA

Copyright © 2007 by Weekly Reader® Early Learning Library

Editor: Barbara Kiely Miller
Art direction: Tammy West
Cover design and page layout: Kami Strunsee
Picture research: Diane Laska-Swanke
Photographs: © John Sibilski Photography

Printed in the United States of America

1 2 3 4 5 6 7 8 9 10 09 08 07 06

Note to Educators and Parents

Reading is such an exciting adventure for young children! They are beginning to integrate their oral language skills with written language. To encourage children along the path to early literacy, books must be colorful, engaging, and interesting; they should invite the young reader to explore both the print and the pictures.

The *My Day at School* series is designed to help young readers review the routines and rules of a school day, while learning new vocabulary and strengthening their reading comprehension. In simple, easy-to-read language, each book follows a child through part of a typical school day.

Each book is specially designed to support the young reader in the reading process. The familiar topics are appealing to young children and invite them to read — and re-read — again and again. The full-color photographs and enhanced text further support the student during the reading process.

In addition to serving as wonderful picture books in schools, libraries, homes, and other places where children learn to love reading, these books are specifically intended to be read within an instructional guided reading group. This small group setting allows beginning readers to work with a fluent adult model as they make meaning from the text. After children develop fluency with the text and content, the book can be read independently. Children and adults alike will find these books supportive, engaging, and fun!

— Susan Nations, M.Ed., author, literacy coach,
and consultant in literacy development

This is my **classroom** at school. I have lots of fun here.

We sit in our chairs. Our teacher calls our names. We are all here today.

We take turns reading.
Our teacher helps us
with hard words.

Then we write our own stories.

I print my story neatly.

Now it is time for **math**. We
are learning to add numbers.
I know the answer.

Then it is time for **science**.
We are learning how
plants grow.

We do different things after lunch. Some days we have art. Today we have music.

We go to the **library**.
My teacher helps me
find a good book.

It is time to go home. I pack my books. See you tomorrow!

Glossary

classroom — a room in a school where classes take place

library — a place that has many books for people to borrow and read

math — short for "mathematics," which is the study of numbers, shapes, and measurements

science — the study of nature and living things

For More Information

Books

The Library. I Like to Visit (series).
Jacqueline Laks Gorman (Gareth Stevens)

Lunch Money and Other Poems About School.
Carol Shields (Puffin)

Teacher. People in My Community (series).
JoAnn Early Macken (Gareth Stevens)

Web Site

Zoom School
www.enchantedlearning.com/school/
Activities, games, and information for school subjects

Publisher's note to educators and parents: Our editors have carefully reviewed this Web site to ensure that it is suitable for children. Many Web sites change frequently, however, and we cannot guarantee that a site's future contents will continue to meet our high standards of quality and educational value. Be advised that children should be closely supervised whenever they access the Internet.

Index

About the Author

Joanne Mattern has written more than one hundred and fifty books for children. Joanne also works in her local library. She lives in New York State with her husband, three daughters, and assorted pets. She enjoys animals, music, going to baseball games, reading, and visiting schools to talk about her books.